Do Your Own

CARAVAN
OR
MOTORHOME

Habitation Check

T0386795

Also from Veloce

Caravan, Improve & Modify Your (Porter)
Caravans, The Illustrated History 1919-1959 (Jenkinson)
Caravans, The Illustrated History From 1960 (Jenkinson)
Dorset from the Sea – The Jurassic Coast from Lyme Regis to Old Harry Rocks photographed from its best viewpoint (also Souvenir Edition) (Belasco)
Drive on the Wild Side, A – 20 Extreme Driving Adventures From Around the World (Weaver)
Essential Guide to Driving in Europe, The (Parish)
France: the essential guide for car enthusiasts – 200 things for the car enthusiast to see and do (Parish)
Micro Caravans (Jenkinson)
Motorhomes – A first-time-buyer's guide (Fry)
Motorhomes, The Illustrated History (Jenkinson)
Renewable Energy Home Handbook, The (Porter)
Roads with a View – England's greatest views and how to find them by road (Corfield)
Sprite Caravans, The Story of (Jenkinson)
Volkswagen Bus Book, The (Bobbitt)
Volkswagen Bus or Van to Camper, How to Convert (Porter)
Volkswagens of the World (Glen)
VW Bay Window Bus, Enthusiast's Restoration Manual (Paxton)
VW Bus – 40 Years of Splitties, Bays & Wedges (Copping)
VW – The Air-cooled Era (Copping)
VW T5 Camper Conversion Manual (Porter)
VW Campers (Copping)
Volkswagen Type 3, The book of the – Concept, Design, International Production Models & Development (Glen)

From Hubble & Hattie

Camper vans, ex-pats and Spanish hounds – The strays of Spain: from road trip to rescue (Coates)
Dogs on wheels – Travelling with your canine companion (Mort)
Emergency first aid for dogs – at home and away (Bucksch)
Walking the dog – Motorway walks for drivers and dogs (Rees)
Wonderful walks from Dog-friendly campsites throughout the UK (Chelmicka)

www.veloce.co.uk

First published in March 2021 by Veloce Publishing Limited, Veloce House, Parkway Farm Business Park, Middle Farm Way, Poundbury, Dorchester DT1 3AR, England. Tel +44 (0)1305 260068 / Fax 01305 250479 / e-mail info@veloce.co.uk / web www.veloce.co.uk or www.velocebooks.com.
ISBN: 978-1-787117-31-0; UPC: 6-36847-01731-6.

Do Your Own

CARAVAN
OR
MOTORHOME
Habitation Check

KEITH SHEPHARD

*Habitation checks are not a legal requirement and do not need
to be carried out by a company. The checks are performed
mainly for motorhome, campervan and caravan owners' peace
of mind, and also to spot problems (and potential problems)
early so as to prevent costly repair bills. Using this book
for guidance, it is possible to carry out your own detailed
habitation checks, saving money year after year.*

VELOCE PUBLISHING
THE PUBLISHER OF FINE AUTOMOTIVE BOOKS

Contents

For Mum, Dad and Rascal.
Gone, but never forgotten – RIP xx

Introduction

Welcome ...

Whether you're a seasoned owner, a complete novice who's new to the world of caravans and motorhomes, a self-build enthusiast, or simply planning to buy your first van, I hope this book will be an invaluable guide. That said, let me introduce myself ...

I have owned a motorcaravan of one form or another for well over two decades. First of all it was just something to holiday in – then it became a hobby – then it became an obsession – then when I started building my own campervans it became a passion!

I cannot think of a time when any of my campers has been in a motorhome workshop. It's not that I have anything against them; it's just that by applying a little common sense, previous experience, some fairly basic DIY skills and a lot of time I have always been able to carry out basic repairs myself, and that is why I am now applying that knowledge to writing this book.

My employment background is in the automotive industry in which I worked for nigh-on 40 years. So, I guess, that gives me a bit of a head start when it comes to carrying out my own repairs by using some previously learned practical skills. At the end of my career I was running my own business which I eventually sold (having received an offer I couldn't refuse) and, as I was in my mid-fifties, I made the decision to retire.

However, early retirement isn't for everybody and I soon became bored. So, I decided to convert a VW Kombi van into a camper that would better suit our needs for the festivals that my wife and I often attend, where there are limited or no electric hook-ups, and also very few shower facilities.

After a month the conversion was completed and we are now able to spend many days off-grid with a gas hob, sink; can run a fridge, microwave and other electrical items which are powered via a good quality 2000 watt inverter that is connected to a large bank of 12-volt batteries.

I also installed a shower in the van, and an electric hook-up point that we can use when mains is available.

Then, for a bit of extra income and something else to do, I began to dabble in camper hire, and this is where the issue of habitation checks became very relevant.

Obviously, when you are hiring out campers, you want to make sure the van is safe for its occupants, that everything is in proper working order, and that the hirers have a trouble-free, enjoyable holiday. Although there's no guarantee that things will always go according to plan (sometimes problems occur that couldn't have been predicted) it was my job, as the hirer, to get the habitation area signed off as safe, damp-free and with all appliances in working order.

Therefore, it was only right that, before starting my hire business, I should look into habitation checks and prices. I found that the average cost of a check is around £200: realising that this would need to be done every year, and that if I wanted to increase my fleet of hire vans this would become a significant extra cost, I began looking into training for the necessary qualification myself. So, after a lot of research, book reading, previously gained knowledge and using my own vans as test dummies I enrolled for the NCC (National Caravan Council) online and practical assessments. I passed the NCC Service Award in 2019 and the rest is history.

Anyway, that's enough about me (do I hear a big sigh of relief?): let's get on with the job in hand …

About this book

This book is for guidance only. The idea is give peace of mind to caravan and motorhome owners that their pride and joy is, to all intents and purposes, fit to stay in. Also, to identify problems early and prevent potential problems before they become costly, disastrous or, worst case scenario, unsolvable.

The book is not intended to be a repair manual and I am not suggesting that anyone takes on a repair task to their caravan or motorhome that may be beyond their skill set or DIY knowledge.

All the information, guidance and test procedures are provided in good faith and to the best of my knowledge are correct at the time of writing.

Over the following pages you will be carrying out checks to the 12-volt leisure battery and the battery charging system.

You will also carry out some basic checks to both the RCD/MCB 230 volt consumer system and the LPG (gas) system. If you have any doubt about your capabilities, or confusion in these areas you should always consult a recognised professional.

You will be checking the operation of the interior appliances, testing for damp, checking the interior and exterior ventilation and the water system.

For caravans and larger motorhomes please be aware that you will be concentrating on interior fixtures and fittings only, and will not be covering checks to the chassis, corner steadies, or any other external feature.

All checks and adjustments to caravan external running gear, couplings, chassis, etc, should always be carried out by a qualified technician.

I will show the tools needed to carry out your checks, where to source them and how to use them, with detailed explanations and pictures.

For owners of newer caravans and motorhomes please be aware that your habitation checks may need to be certified by an approved workshop to cover any existing warranty issues. But, in all cases, this book will still come in useful for periodic checking of your caravan's appliances and equipment, and give everyone who reads it an improved working knowledge of how their caravan or motorhome functions.

The book and its contents will also be of great value for anyone thinking of purchasing their first caravan or motorhome because, after all, as a caravan or motorhome will be one of the largest purchases that anyone undertakes, if problems can be identified at the point of sale it will save the inconvenience of having to return your vehicle to the seller at a later date, and maybe having to argue your case over issues that should have been put right before you handed over your hard-earned cash.

NB. If, when carrying out your tests, problems are identified with the 230-volt electrical system or LPG gas system, subsequent repairs should always be carried out by a competent and suitably qualified technician.

1 What is a habitation check and why do I need one?

✓ To ensure the interior of your motorhome or caravan is safe for you and any other occupants

✓ For peace of mind

✓ To spot potential problems early

✓ Spotting problems early will prevent them becoming more costly

✓ To spot potential issues that may affect the warranty on newer vehicles*

✓ Lack of maintenance will void your warranty

✓ To make sure all appliances and equipment are working correctly

✓ To enjoy your holidays and lessen the risk of equipment/appliance breakdowns

✓ To protect your investment

✓ A regular habitation check schedule will help to maintain the value of your vehicle

✓ To save money by doing it yourself

*Check with your dealer what needs to be done to satisfy your warranty terms and conditions.

2 What tools will I need, where can I buy them and how much will they cost?

For general use
Hand tools
Most people will have a basic set of spanners and screwdrivers for general maintenance around the home; these are handy for accessing equipment inside your caravan or motorhome that may be hidden behind panels or trim. If not, these can be purchased very cheaply from your local DIY store or online. So, let's say £20.

The most commonly used spanners are 10mm and 13mm.

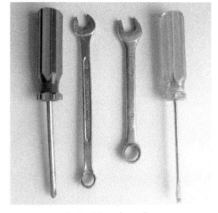
2-1. Hand tools.

Electrical testing
Multimeter
You will need a multimeter to test the leisure battery voltage, the battery charging system, and for checking the condition of the vehicle electric hook-up point and cable.

You will need a multimeter that measures ohms for any tests on the electric hook-up facility of your vehicle. A good quality multimeter can be purchased on sites such as eBay or Amazon for as little as £10.

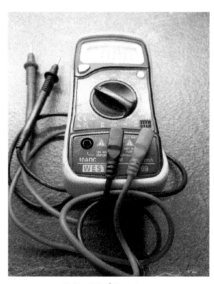
2-2. Multimeter.

Gas leak testing

LPG/combustible gas leak detector

I bought one of these Smart Sensors on eBay (they also come in red) for under £20. It has visual and audible warning functions and works very well.

The unit was supplied with a decent set of instructions and is extremely easy to use. You'll need one of these to check for any escaping gas around the gas bottle, pipe work and appliances.

Damp testing

Moisture/damp tester

There are two main types of damp tester. The one pictured opposite is a probed type damp tester, which can be bought very cheaply on eBay or Amazon.

However, if you do choose to buy the probe type you will need to dig into your vehicle's interior panels, which can cause visible marks and/or small holes. Probe type testers can be bought for as little as £10.

In my opinion it's worth spending a bit more and buying an Intelligent Moisture Meter such as the one in picture 2.4, because it doesn't use probes.

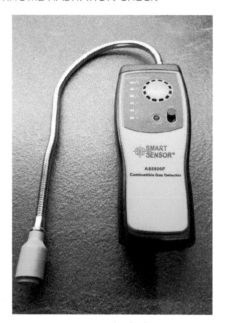

2-3. LPG gas leak detector.

2-4. Intelligent moisture meter.

The meter is simply offered against the vehicle interior panels and woodwork to obtain a reading and thus is completely non-invasive. The unit also has a high level of accuracy.

I purchased my Intelligent Moisture Meter for £30 on Amazon.

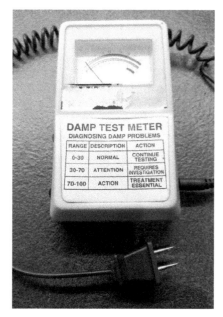

2-5. Moisture meter with probes.

Equipment summary
HAND TOOLS: £20 (you may have these in your toolbox already)
MULTIMETER: £10 (make sure it has voltage and ohms settings)
GAS LEAK DETECTOR: £20 (easily sourced online)
INTELLIGENT MOISTURE/DAMP METER: £30 (search on eBay or Amazon. The cheaper probe type tester can be bought for around £10, but this will leave marks in the vehicle's interior panels)

TOTAL COST OF EQUIPMENT = £80
AVERAGE COST OF A HABITATION CHECK = £200
YOUR SAVING = £120
And you can use your equipment year after year!

3 **In the beginning ...**

Okay, let's assume you have all your equipment to hand now. This is not an absolute essential at this stage – you don't have to have bought it yet – you may want to just continue reading to see if the following pages and guides are within your skill set before making any purchases, which is fine.

I'm not suggesting that anyone should continue with anything in this book they are unsure about; if in doubt always contact a suitably qualified professional. If you should decide that some of the checks and tests are beyond your capabilities then at least you will have gained some knowledge, so if you decide to call in a professional you will have some idea of what they will be looking for, and be more comfortable with some of the jargon that may be used.

I have tried to make everything as straightforward as possible by using terminology that is easy to understand, and by using images to make all the check procedures as clear as possible, and I hope I have succeeded!

Before you start checking stuff on the inside you're going to have a look at the outside. If I was carrying out a habitation check for a paying customer I would be noting down and taking photos of the bodywork to record any dents, scratches, damaged trims or blemishes. This is firstly to protect myself from the customer coming back to me at a later date claiming that the damage wasn't there before I started work on the vehicle, and secondly to record any damaged panels or exterior trims that may be letting in water (water ingress), which could potentially cause damp problems on the inside. Be aware that mouldy or dirt-blocked trims will cause water build-up, so (being as this is your own lovely caravan or motorhome you're dealing with) it's a good idea to clean up or unblock any suspect areas before moving on to the interior fixtures and fittings.

At this point, it's beneficial to make some simple sketches of the front, rear and both sides of your vehicle, for future reference. With these you will be able mark down on the relevant panel any problems that may need attention now or in the near future.

The vehicle sketches will also come in useful later in the book in Chapter 10, Damp testing, to record your readings for each individual interior area.

Use a notebook to record your findings on all equipment and appliances as you work your way through the book. Start a new page for every section you complete, and use the appropriate heading.

Or, if you want to be really clever and professional, you could devise your own tick box checklist.

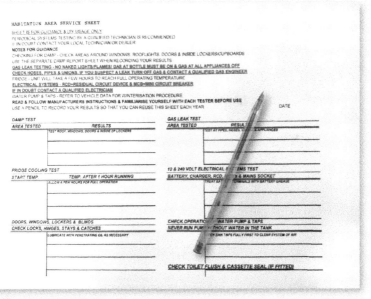

An example checklist, a larger version is shown on page 58 if you'd like to make a copy.

4 The order of service

There is no particular order in which you must carry out your motorhome/caravan habitation check, but personally I always begin with testing the condition of the leisure battery. My reasoning is that as the leisure battery is the power source for the entire 12V direct current (DC) electrical system, before testing anything else it seems to make sense to ensure the leisure battery is in good condition first.

Otherwise, if the battery is in a discharged state or at the end of its useful life, when we come to test 12V appliances such as the water pump, lights, etc, they may not perform properly, and could give a false impression of their condition and/or functionality that may lead to confusion or possibly unnecessary replacement costs.

Right, now that's clear let's get checking ...

The leisure battery: a good place to start.

5 The leisure (habitation) battery

Testing and leisure battery condition

For this test you will need your multimeter.

The red lead of your multimeter should be plugged in to the VΩmA socket on your device, and the black lead into the COM socket: this will be the same for all tests carried out here and later in this book. Now switch it on to voltage.

Depending on what multimeter you have, there can be up to three voltage settings. The one you need to select for these tests is the 20V option (usually the middle setting), as nothing you find here should read more than 20V.

Once you have located your leisure battery, which could be in the engine bay (as the one I'm testing is), under the cab seats, or hidden away in an interior cabinet, depending on the build of your caravan or motorhome, carry out a visual check of its condition:

☑ Check the battery terminals and clamps are clean, tight, and free from corrosion.
☑ Check the condition of the battery leads, and that none of the protective insulation is bare or broken.
☑ Check the battery is properly secured and can't slide about in its compartment.
☑ Check the battery compartment is secure and that gas from the battery can't escape into the habitation area.
☑ Check the battery outer casing for signs of distortion/bulging which may have been caused by overheating or neglect.

The majority of leisure batteries sold these days will be maintenance-free/sealed types, so I'm not going into detail about topping-up of conventional, older style batteries as there is plenty of information on the web about how to do this if need be. But, in short, if the battery stoppers/caps can be removed, the electrolyte should be covering the top of the battery plates by ¼ inch. Use distilled water if topping-up is needed – don't use battery acid!

- Protective gloves should be worn (rubber is ideal) when handling lead-acid batteries.

- Should you need to disconnect the leisure battery at any point, either for maintenance or replacement, always disconnect the negative (-) lead first and the positive (+) last.
  When reconnecting it's the other way round, connect the positive (+) lead first and the negative (-) last.

- If signs of acid corrosion are present (white powdery stuff) remove the battery and/or battery tray and clean using hot water. Once done check for acid leakage and that the battery is properly ventilated.

- Specialist battery clamp grease to prevent acid corrosion from reoccurring can be purchased online or at your local motorist store.

When you have completed the visual inspection, test the leisure battery voltage by touching the red lead of your multimeter to the positive terminal of the battery, and the black lead to the negative terminal.

A good reading here would be 12.6V or above. If the voltage is below this, but above 11.8V, I would suggest removing the battery for recharging. If the voltage is below 11.8V it's quite possible the battery needs replacing, and it's probably worth taking it to your local battery specialist for further testing.

As you can see from image 5-1 the leisure battery voltage is at 12.78V, which is a healthy reading.

5-1. Leisure battery voltage test.

6 The vehicle charging system

Testing leisure battery voltage with the engine running
While you've got your multimeter out we're going to have a look at the vehicle charging system. This is also referred to as the split charge system. The idea is while you're travelling between campsites the charging system of the vehicle will charge not only the vehicle starter battery, but also the leisure battery via the alternator – hence the term split charge.

Earlier vehicles will most likely be fitted with a split charge relay that is fitted to the circuit between the alternator and the starter and leisure batteries.

On newer vehicles, such as those with the latest Euro 5 and 6 engines, a different type of split charge system needs to be used, such as a DC battery charger, also referred to as a battery-to-battery charger. This is because these later, low emission engines are commonly fitted with regenerative braking systems and smart alternators with which conventional split charge relays will not work correctly. DC battery chargers are also far more efficient and quicker at charging the leisure battery than relays.

Pictured is the DC battery charger fitted to one of my own campers. Image 6-1 is of the unit in sleep mode (engine off) and 6-2 is with the unit operating (engine on).

As you can see from image 6-2 the voltage displayed is 14.2V with the engine running, which is just about spot on! You will be looking for a similar reading when you conduct your test.

Anyway, that's enough about split charging because for the purposes of this book that's probably already more than you need to know right now.

For the check I'm going to assume that you don't have a unit with a

6-1. DC charger in sleep mode ... and 6-2. with engine running.

display such as the one above, and you'll be doing the check with your multimeter. So, please continue as follows:

- Start your vehicle.
- Make sure your multimeter is still on the 20V setting.
- Connect the multimeter to the leisure battery (red probe to battery positive (+), black to battery negative (−)).
- A good voltage reading should be 14-14.5V (see image 6-3, overleaf).
- A lower reading, say below 13.8V, may mean that either the split charging system or the alternator is not working properly, and may require further testing by a competent workshop or garage.

You may also have an onboard battery charger fitted to your vehicle which you can use to recharge your leisure battery while it's connected to a campsite or domestic electric hook-up facility. We will cover this unit later on in the book when the vehicle is connected to the mains.

For now, take a break, have a cup of tea and give yourself a pat on the back.

6-3. Split charge system check.

7 The mains electrical (AC) system

Okay, so you're suitably refreshed, very pleased with yourself and ready to carry on with the job in hand. Now you're going to learn a little about ohms (look for this symbol on your multimeter Ω).

If you took physics at school then you may well be familiar with ohms. If you didn't then I'm not about to give you a physics lesson because, to be quite honest, I didn't exactly see eye to eye with my physics teacher, and that didn't bode well with regards to my exam result.

Basically Ohm's law is all about resistance in a circuit, and you're going to use ohms to test the resistance in your electric hook-up extension cable and visually check the hook-up point on your vehicle. For this check, the higher the resistance the better.

That explained let's continue ...

- Turn your multimeter back on. Leave the leads connected to the multimeter set up exactly the same as when you did your voltage tests, and turn the dial round to the ohms Ω setting.
- Depending on what make of multimeter you have there might be more than one ohms setting (20k, 200k and 2M) or the meter might just set ohms automatically. Whatever type of meter you have you should now set it to the maximum, which, in my case, is 2M.
- Again, depending on the brand of multimeter, once you switch it round to ohms the display will show 1 or OL (open loop) which means the resistance in the circuit is infinite and the meter is unable to register because it has reached its maximum range as in image 7-1 on the next page.
- To check your multimeter is functioning correctly, take both probes

and touch them together. You should now have a reading of 000, which means between the leads of the multimeter itself there is no resistance; that's exactly the reading you want and means you can carry on. See image 7-2.

- Firstly, check the condition of the plugs at each end of the hook-up cable and check that they are free from damage, dirt or corrosion. Secondly, you should do a visual check along the complete length of your hook-up lead and look for any breaks or splits in its insulated covering. If any damage is found the whole cable should be replaced.

- Now you're going to check for resistance at each end of your hook-up extension lead.

- Touch the multimeter probes between the plug pins of one end of your hook-up lead (it doesn't matter which way round you connect the probes – red and black are irrelevant

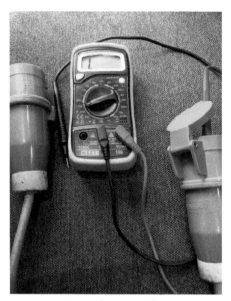

7-1. Multimeter ohms.

7-2. Continuity.

7-3. Resistance.

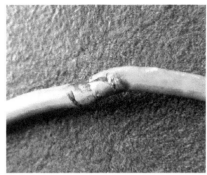

7-4. This hook-up cable has damage to the outer insulation.

7-5. Hook-up point condition.

in this test) your multimeter display should read maximum resistance (see image 7-3).

- This tells us the pins of the hook-up lead are adequately insulated, not going to short-circuit, and that all is well.
- Repeat the test between the plug pins at the other end of the cable.
- Image 7-4 shows obvious damage to a cable that should be replaced.
- Visually check the condition of the vehicle's hook-up point. If there are signs of damage, visible cracks, or signs of overheating then the hook-up point should be replaced.

I said I wasn't going to give a physics lesson, but I've just had a visit from Mr Conroy (my teacher) from beyond the grave, who insisted I show you more.

The following sequence of images shows a test on a fused piece of wire.

- With the black meter probe not connected to the wire it shows infinite resistance.

7-6. Resistance test.

- When the black lead is connected the meter displays 000 resistance and that there is continuity through the wire.

7-7. Continuity test.

- Once the fuse is removed there is infinite resistance again because the circuit has been broken.

7-8. Fuse removed.

- With the fuse back in there's no resistance once more.

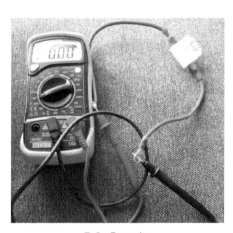

7-9. Fuse in.

Not only does this sequence demonstrate the basics of resistance and continuity, it also demonstrates the importance of fuses in an electrical circuit. Fuses are there to break the circuit should an electrical fault occur, by blowing when a current overload happens. You will read more about the importance of fuses later on in the book.

Are you happy now Mr Conroy? I don't know why we didn't get along really, because I'm such a nice guy – aren't I?

If you've found no problems with your hook-up lead or vehicle hook-up point it's time to plug in and move on.

If you're doing this at home (as I suppose most people will be), and if you don't already have one, you'll need an adapter such as the one on the right, so that you can connect to your home mains supply.

RCD and MCBs
- RCD is the abbreviation for residual current device.
- MCB is the abbreviation for miniature circuit breaker.

7-10. Mains lead adapter.

It's very likely you'll have an RCD unit somewhere in your caravan/motorhome. If you haven't, then either you haven't got mains electric, or your vehicle is a deathtrap!

In most cases the RCD will look something like the one in image 7-11. It might be smaller, or it might be bigger, depending on how many plug outlets and electric appliances you have fitted to your vehicle. But, in this particular case, size doesn't matter as their operation is basically the same.

7-11. RCD unit.

7-12. This control panel has an integrated battery charger.

7-13. Control panel with integral RCD and MCBs.

The stand-alone RCD unit pictured in image 7-11 is separate from the vehicle's control panel, and the unit will usually be located in a cupboard, wardrobe or locker.

The control panel in image 7-12 is an integrated power distribution unit that houses a mains supply for the battery charger (as mentioned in Chapter 5 – there will be more on this and how to check it is functioning properly later in this chapter), as well as a separate 12V cigar lighter socket, and the 12V controls for the fridge and water pump, with the relevant 12V fuses.

The purpose of the RCD is to protect you and other occupants of the vehicle from a major electrical short-circuit and possible electrocution. In a similar vein, the MCBs in your system are designed to protect individual circuits and appliances from electrical current overload. Carry out a visual check of both the RCD and MCBs, making sure that they are in good condition and free of damage or corrosion.

Your vehicle should now be plugged into the mains electric supply via your hook-up cable, so switch the RCD and MCBs to the on position (the blue and white buttons on these models, respectively).

Now you should locate the test button (blue in the model pictured in image 7-11, but on other models it could be yellow or orange) and press it. The RCD should trip out to the 'off' position in a millisecond if everything is working okay. If not, contact a qualified electrician before going any further.

If the RCD unit does what it should, you can continue to check the operation of other electrical appliances and plug sockets.

For complete peace of mind with regards to your vehicle's plug sockets, purchase a socket tester (available online or at your local electrical retailer) which should only set you back around £10.

Should you decide to splash out on that socket tester

7-14. Socket tester with plug switched off, and ... 7-15. ... switched on.

(recommended), results with the plug switched off and on should look something like that in images 7-14 and 7-15.

The three LEDs that have lit up in image 7-15 indicate that there is a good earth, no reverse polarity is present, and that all is good.

Now it's time to revisit caravan and motorhome charging systems as I mentioned earlier. Remember that talk about an onboard charger? Well, it's time to grab your multimeter again and switch it back to the 20V setting.

7-16. Reich Impulse leisure battery charger.

It's possible that your vehicle may not have an onboard charging facility (some lower specification conversions won't), but if it does it might look something like the one in image 7-16. Alternatively, if you have an all-singing, all-dancing control panel that houses both the mains electrical and 12V electrical systems, the charger is likely to be housed somewhere in the control panel unit itself.

If you're unsure about whether you have an onboard battery charger, or you're having problems locating the charger unit or switch, consult the company that built your caravan or motorhome.

I fitted a Reich Impulse charger to my campervan conversion. This is a 10 amp, fully automatic leisure battery charger, which, if all is working correctly, will cut out when the optimum battery voltage is reached and thus will not over-charge the leisure battery.

• So, for the purposes of this check we're going to assume you've now switched on the battery charger.
• Next, let's go back to the leisure battery and carry out another voltage test by connecting the multimeter to the leisure battery

terminals exactly as you did in Chapter 5, but this time you're looking for a different voltage reading.

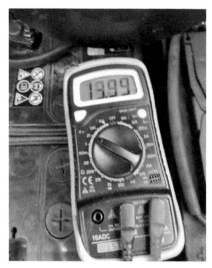

7-17. Battery charger voltage.

- If battery voltage has increased to about 13.6V or above, the charger is working. If the voltage is well below 13.6V the charger isn't functioning properly, if at all. And, similarly, if the voltage rises above 14.6V, it's likely the unit is charging too high (over-charging). In this case the charger will cause damage to the leisure battery, make it hot to the touch after a short time, run the risk of excessive battery gassing (lead-acid batteries generate hydrogen gas) and possible explosion. If in doubt contact the manufacturer of your onboard battery charger for advice.
- In the test shown in image 7-17 I have a voltage reading just below 14V: this means my onboard battery charger is working correctly.

Right, now that's sorted, it's time to turn the fridge to its electric function and pop in a beer that, hopefully, will be cold enough to have as a celebratory drink by the time you finish the rest of your checks!

☺ Isn't electricity wonderful? One day, I decided to pretend that my old car was a newer electric model. So, I put some earplugs in, drove it around for a while and then pushed it home.

8 The 12-volt (DC) electrical system

The 12-volt leisure battery system

By now you should have established that your leisure battery is in good working condition. It is very important for this section that the leisure battery is in a satisfactory, charged state in order to test the appliances that run off 12V (the leisure battery system).

8-1. A typical 12V control panel.

As stated in the previous section, your caravan or motorhome may have a control panel that integrates the 230V electrical system (mains) and the 12V electrical system in the same unit. Either way, whether your 12V system is housed in an integrated unit or a separate unit, the 12V side of things will probably look something similar to the panel pictured above.

It may seem to many readers like stating the bleeding obvious (forgive me if that's the case, but I'm assuming there are some uninitiated campers out there who have chosen to purchase this book) to point out that the switch on the left is the on/off switch. Here you can select whether you wish to obtain the 12V power from the vehicle starter battery (car) or the leisure battery (van). Depending on the

8-2. This 12V control panel has a fresh water gauge.

control panel brand the wording might be slightly different – such as starter and leisure options – but their meanings are the same.

For 99.9% of the time it is sensible to select the leisure battery option. The only reason to select the starter battery option would be if the leisure battery is totally discharged and some emergency 12V power is needed for a short period of time. Running your 12V appliances from the starter battery for long periods will inevitably result in a vehicle that doesn't start because of a discharged battery.

The 12V control panel in image 8-2 refers to the leisure battery selection as HAB (an abbreviation of habitation) and the starter battery as VEHICLE. It also has a separate MASTER switch that must be turned on before either battery can be selected.

To measure the state of charge of your batteries select either HAB or VEHICLE and press the BATTERY switch (middle left), and the unit will indicate battery voltage.

As well as a battery condition monitor, this particular unit has an option to measure the onboard water tank level.

Press the WATER switch (middle right) and if you have water in your onboard tank you should get a reading. If you know you have a good quantity of water in the tank (ie, half a tank or more) and the meter still shows empty then either the tank sensor is faulty or the water indicator switch needs calibrating.

If you can't get a battery voltage reading from either battery when selected this would indicate the fuse from the battery to the panel has blown (see the next page), a possible wiring fault or the control panel itself is faulty.

The 12V battery fuses

Assuming your caravan or motorhome is wired correctly, both the starter battery and the leisure battery cables that lead to the 12V control panel will be fused.

In image 8-3, which came from an Auto-Sleeper Trident based on the VW Transporter, the battery fuses are situated in the engine bay. As the starter battery and leisure battery sit side by side under the bonnet, this is the sensible option.

8-3. Battery fuses (under the bonnet in this case).

The rating of the battery fuses will depend on how many 12V appliances you have.

For smaller campers with only a few 12V appliances, a 30 amp fuse would probably suffice, and for larger motorhomes with more 12V equipment, the battery fuses could be as high as 40, 50 or 60 amps. Basically, the battery fuses should be of a rating that will be able to cope without the fuse blowing in the event you choose to run all the 12V appliances at the same time.

Due to the vast array of caravan and motorhome converters out there it's impossible to list the battery fuse location for every vehicle.

Saying that, as a rule of thumb, the fuse would usually be located somewhere reasonably near to the battery itself. But, please be aware that the fuse shouldn't be positioned in the battery compartment, because the spark caused in the event of a fuse blowing could cause an explosion. As explained earlier, lead-acid batteries generate hydrogen gas.

Once you've found the battery fuses they should be checked for corrosion and any signs of damage or over-heating.

While you're there, check the cables themselves for any damage to their insulated covering that might have been caused by chafing or bad routing.

One more thing to bear in mind about the 12V electrics is that if any cables run through the LPG gas bottle compartment, they should be protected by gas-tight conduit or ducting.

12V control panel and fuses

If you read Chapter 6 of this book and followed the continuity/resistance test I demonstrated by removing the fuse from a length of cable, you will be familiar with the function of fuses.

Fuses are probably the most important part of any 12V electrical installation. Without a properly rated fuse that will blow should a circuit become overloaded, there is a risk of burning cables, and possibly fire.

Image 8-4 shows a 12V control panel with the fuse holders removed.

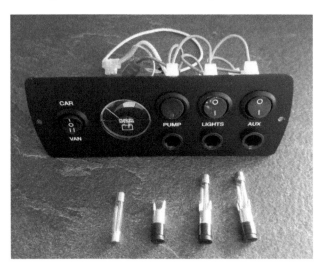

8-4. 12V control panel with integrated fuse holders.

On this particular model the fuse holders and the fuses can be inspected by a simple half turn with a flat blade screwdriver. The switch for each circuit (PUMP, LIGHTS and AUX) is protected by a 10-amp glass fuse (different models might use blade type fuses).

Carry out a visual inspection of the fuse holders for cracks or corrosion, and check that the fuses are not blown by looking for breaks in the wire.

If you suspect a fuse is seriously over-rated, for example a 30-amp fuse is where a 10-amp fuse should be, this might indicate a possible fault in the circuit that has caused a correctly rated fuse to continuously blow because of current overload. Try the circuit with a correctly rated fuse: if it blows further investigation is required.

If your eyesight is starting to fail, like mine is, then a battery, bulb and fuse tester is an excellent addition to your toolbox. These cost very little and are great for use around the home, too!

You can see an example in image 8-5.

When a 12V appliance or piece of equipment seems to have no power going to it, the most sensible and time-saving option is to first check the relevant fuse.

8-5. Testing a fuse – this one is okay.

So, now that you've established that the fuses in your control panel are in good condition and correctly rated (if you have the original conversion owner's manual you can refer to this), it's time to check that the water pump, lights, and any other 12V auxiliaries are functioning properly. I won't go into detail here because it's all pretty self-explanatory.

12V fridge operation
Two main types of refrigerators are used in caravans and motorhomes:

Absorption fridge
This type of fridge has no moving parts other than the refrigerant itself, and changes the gas back into a liquid by applying heat generated from either gas or electric power. They are often referred to as 'three-way fridges,' and can work on either gas or electric from a 12V or 230V mains power supply.

The fact that they run silently makes them ideal for use in leisure vehicles and boats.

Compressor fridge
These are much like smaller versions of your fridge at home, and, as the name implies, they use a compressor to pump refrigerant through the system. They can also be known as 'two-way fridges,' and will usually run on either a 12V or mains electric supply.

They are noisier than absorption fridges, which can be a problem in smaller caravans, especially when trying to sleep. Although, due to continuing advances in technology, the noise aspect is not such an issue in the latest models.

Modern caravan and motorhome converters are increasingly turning to compressor type fridges that don't need venting, but older conversions will most likely be fitted with absorption, three-way fridges.

8-6. A typical three-way fridge.

As compressor fridges need

very little maintenance, in this section I'm going to concentrate on absorption fridges and the three-way function.

Because they can run off gas and also generate quite a lot of heat, absorption type fridges need proper ventilation to the outside.

It's time now to switch off the fridge mains switch (green on the model pictured below), and turn on the engine.

• The red switch on the far left is the 12V switch and should now be switched to 'on.' The 12V operation of the fridge only works with the engine running, and is controlled by means of its own, separate relay.

8-7. A three-way fridge with the engine off.

8-8. Engine on and three-way fridge running on 12V power supply.

• If all is functioning as it should the red switch will illuminate to show that the power supply is good. If there's no illumination then you have a problem either with the fuse (usually found by the fridge relay), the wiring, a faulty relay or the fridge itself.

• While concentrating on the fridge it would seem a good idea to check the gas operation, too.

• Switch off your vehicle and the 12V fridge function. Now go outside and take a look at the fridge ventilation. Make sure the vents are clear of debris and mould and are in good condition.

• When you've established the vents are clear and are in good order the next thing to do is test the gas operation.

• Turn on your gas bottle, and make sure that the vehicle is switched on at the 12V control panel, as you'll need power for the gas ignition switch.

- Turn the gas knob on the fridge to its maximum flame position, press the knob in to allow gas flow and turn the ignition switch to on.

- The ignition switch should flash to begin with, and then stop flashing after a few seconds to confirm that the gas has ignited and the fridge is now running. If the light doesn't go off and is continuously flashing, there's a problem with the ignition.

8-9. Typical three-way fridge ventilation.

- Once the fridge is lit you should see a nice blue flame through the inspection hole at the back of the unit, as indicated in image 8-11. If the flame is yellow and/ or sputtering, the gas isn't burning properly and the fridge needs

attention from a suitably qualified engineer.

- Now go back to the gas bottle and switch off the gas. After a short time when the gas supply is completely cut off the ignition light should start flashing again. This is a built-in safety feature, and is a good sign because it means the fridge is trying to re-ignite itself

8-10. Igniting the gas operation on a three-way fridge.

8-11. The fridge should run with a blue flame, which can be seen through the inspection hole.

now that it senses the flame has gone out.

For absorption fridges to work properly the vehicle must be on reasonably level ground.

Okay, you're done with the gas operation of the fridge, so switch the fridge back onto mains electric, and keep chilling that beer for later on.

We're now going to look at the LPG system in more depth ...

9 The liquefied petroleum gas (LPG) system

The LPG locker and components
Innovative products on the leisure vehicle and marine market can cut out the need for LPG entirely. Many appliances that did run on LPG, such as hobs and interior heating systems are now available to run off the vehicle diesel tank.

Also, advances in lithium battery technology means that a very powerful battery bank, half the size and weight of conventional lead-acid batteries, can be linked together to run electric hobs and other appliances.

However, alternative systems to LPG can be very costly, and therefore gas systems are still, by far, more prevalent.

9-1. A typical gas locker compartment.

If you spot or suspect a problem with the LPG system, any necessary repairs *should only be carried out by an LPG qualified technician.*

LPG is highly flammable, so it goes without saying the while working around it there should be no smoking or naked flames.

In the last section you tested the operation of the three-way fridge on gas, so now you're going to move on the other LPG appliances. But, there are a few preliminary checks to the LPG system itself that need to be carried out first:

☑ Check the gas locker is properly vented and the vents are clear. Liquefied petroleum gas is heavier than air so the vents should be situated at the lowest point of the gas locker.

☑ Make sure the gas bottle itself is free of damage, no corrosion is present, is of the right size for the gas locker and able to stand upright freely.

9-2. Gas locker ventilation.

☑ Check the gas regulator is the right type (ie red for propane gas and blue for butane gas), check there is no visible damage, and, if possible, its age. Regulators have a recommended service life of ten years. The propane regulator pictured has a date of manufacture stamped on it (10 14 = October 2014).

☑ Check the condition of the flexible hose and that there are no signs of cracking or deterioration. Check the date of manufacture printed

9-3. This Calor gas regulator has the date of manufacture as 10 14.

on the hose. The jury's still out on this, but the general consensus is that if the hose is older than five years then replacement is recommended. The gas hose pictured has a manufacture date of 07/17.

☑ Check that the gas locker is in good condition and that the bottle can be properly secured in place with a strap or similar.

9-4. This gas hose was manufactured in July 2017.

Now it's time to get out your gas leak detector and calibrate it as per the instruction manual.

As you're now in the vicinity of the gas locker, regulator and hose, this would seem an excellent place to start.

- Use the detector to check around the regulator, along the hose, and any joins especially.
- Your detector should stay quiet and with no lights showing. If it screams at you and lights up like a Christmas tree, switch off the gas very quickly, run away, and get on the phone to a qualified LPG technician!
- If you didn't have to run away, use the detector to check

9-5. Checking for gas leaks around the regulator and hose.

around all gas valves and visible pipework.

- Notice that there is another gas drop-out vent underneath the valves and pipes on the model pictured in image 9-6.
- Visually check the gas pipe earth connection to the chassis for damage or corrosion, and make sure it is tight and sound.

All being well you can continue with checking the LPG appliances.

LPG heaters and water heaters
It is beyond the scope of this book to carry out servicing or repairs to interior heaters and water heaters (if fitted). If you have LPG heating appliances in your vehicle, it is a requirement that they should be serviced at regular intervals, and any subsequent repairs must be carried out by a competent, qualified technician.

9-6. Gas valves and ventilation.

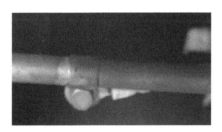

9-7. A typical gas pipe earth connection.

You can, however, carry out some basic routines:

☑ Check that the appliance ignites in good time.

☑ If the appliance has an inspection window where the shape and colour of the flame can be seen, check that the flame is constant and blue in colour (as you did with the three-way fridge).

☑ Check that the heating appliance works in accordance with the manufacturer's manual.

☑ Visually check that the outside exhaust flue outlets are clear, in good condition, unobstructed and that there are not excessive sooty deposits around them that might indicate unburned gas and, more seriously, carbon monoxide.

🔍 For complete peace of mind the LPG system should be periodically pressure tested by an LPG certified technician.

9-8. LPG heater exhaust.

LPG hobs, grills and ovens

Here you will be visually checking that the flame of the cooking appliances is the correct shape and colour, and, later on, the operation of their respective flame failure device (FFD).

First of all you're going to look at the flame on the hob. So, switch on one of the burners and light it. The burner should ignite quickly and the flame should be constant and blue in colour with no sputtering.

- The flame pictured in image 9-9 is blue and constant, which is perfect.
- If the flame is yellow and/ or sputtering occurs, there is a problem with the gas combustion.
- Poor combustion could be caused by something as simple

9-9. This burner has a nice blue flame.

as a dirty or blocked burner, and a good clean might clear the problem. But, if cleaning fails to remedy the problem the appliance shouldn't be used until an LPG qualified technician has been consulted.

- Repeat this test with the other burners, grill, and oven if fitted.

Flame failure device (FFD)

The FFD is a safety feature fitted to all gas appliances so that the gas flow to the appliance is shut off if the flame goes out, and to prevent a build-up of carbon monoxide and poisoning that could be caused by unburned gas.

If you have gas appliances around your home you can carry out the FFD check on them, too.

Open a door or large window when performing the FFD test.

It's time to bring your gas leak detector to hand once more and, again, this test should be repeated on each burner in turn, the grill and the oven.

- Light the appliance and then extinguish the flame. When the flame has gone out, place the gas detector over the appliance gas jet.
- This is the time when your detector *should* be screaming at you and lighting up like a Christmas tree (see image 9-10), but don't run away this time,

9-10. Begin testing the FFDs.

because this is how it should be and you're not finished yet.

- Now move the detector away from the gas jet and step away from the appliance.
- If the FFD is working correctly you should hear a click after about 20-30 seconds when the FFD shuts off the gas flow. If it fails to shut off in a reasonable time then the FFD is faulty.
- Assuming that the FFD has done its job, allow the gas to escape for a minute or two via an open door or window. Then return your detector to the gas jet: all should be quiet and Christmas will be over.

9-11. The FFD is working correctly.

My word, aren't FFDs just so much fun? I bet you can hardly contain yourself, can you? But we must leave them now, as we're approaching the end of the habitation check, and that cold beer awaits ...

For the next section, if you did the sketches of the front, back and sides of your vehicle that I mentioned in Chapter 3, it's time to drag them out because you'll need them for the damp testing.

☺ When I dragged out my old sketch pad from the drawer I found an old letter from my wife from when we were courting. It was just a blank piece of paper, which seemed strange at first ... but then I remembered we weren't speaking at the time.

10 Damp testing (water ingress)

Condensation versus damp

So, you've got your A4 pad to hand, and if you're as bad at sketching as I am (and depending on the size/shape of your vehicle) you may well have something that looks like the image below.

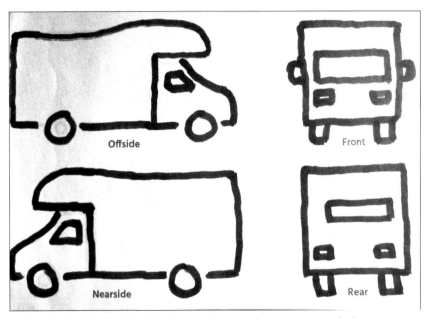

10-1. A badly-sketched motorhome – hope you can do better!

Just to clarify, the things that are sticking out the sides of the front view aren't funny ears, they're wing mirrors.

It doesn't matter how rough your sketch is as long as you understand it.

First of all you're going to do a weather check. Weather conditions are important because you don't want to confuse condensation with damp.

This is especially relevant if your caravan or motorhome has been laid up for a while, eg over the winter months. If that's the case it's a good idea to give it a good airing by opening the doors and windows for a while before damp testing.

Also, try to pick a reasonable day when the weather conditions aren't too dank.

As you carry out your interior damp tests, mark the area with an 'X' in the appropriate position on your sketches and also write down the resulting damp/moisture meter readings.

Moisture meter readings and what they mean

Image 10-2 shows a reading I took with the moisture meter resting on a damp sheet of kitchen towel, giving a reading of 35%.

If you record any readings like this anywhere around your vehicle you should either push your vehicle over a cliff or prepare yourself for a hefty repair bill.

Below is a list of moisture readings and what they say about the damp tightness of your vehicle.

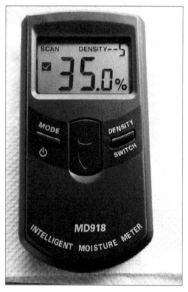

- **0-15% = Good.** This means there's nothing to worry about.

- **16-20% = Average.** This suggests it might be a good idea to carry out another test in a few months just to keep a close eye on things.

- **21-25% = Suspicious.** This would indicate that water ingress

10-2. Intelligent moisture meter reading.

is possibly in progress, and further investigation may be required. Performing a visual check in the particular area might reveal more.

- **26-30% = Bad.** Water ingress is in progress and repair work and associated costs are inevitable.

- **31% or higher = Very bad**. There is most likely structural damage; the area requires a full strip down and potentially very expensive repairs.

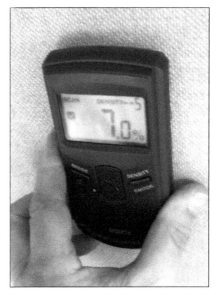

10-3. Damp testing the upper interior panels.

Where to damp test

You should carry out damp testing to the following areas in particular:

- The vehicle ceiling.
- The upper parts of the interior panels just below where they meet the ceiling.
- Around windows.
- Cupboards and wardrobes.
- Doors.
- Roof vents and other apertures.
- Around sinks, water pipes and other water fixtures.
- The floor.

Products available for repairing worn or leaking seals around doors and windows come in liquid form, and will fill hairline cracks.

One such product is called 'Creeping Crack Cure,' which reminds me of a true story from when I was running my shop ...

☺ One day an older couple came into the shop and began browsing the motorhome product shelves. The man picked up a bottle of Creeping Crack Cure, turned to his wife and said, "You could do with some of this!" ... and that's when the fight started.

11 Ventilation and internal condition

If you have followed this book to the letter, you should have checked the exterior fridge vents in Chapter 8, and both the LPG heater and water heater vents in Chapter 9.

If you decided to skip that part then you should do it now:

☑ Check that all exterior vents and exhaust flues are not blocked, are in good condition, and don't have excessive sooty deposits that might indicate poor combustion.

☑ Making sure that any interior vents are clear and unobstructed is important, not only to disperse smells and moisture, but also to expel the small amounts of carbon dioxide/carbon monoxide that result from cooking on LPG appliances.

☑ As well as fixed interior vents, check the operation of windows, roof vents and doors.

☑ Check the interior fixtures, appliances, and panels, and that cupboard/wardrobe doors close properly and are secure.

☑ Check the operation of curtains, window blinds and fly screens.

💡 While you're walking around inside your caravan or motorhome test the floor for sponginess.

Excessive movement might indicate delamination, which happens when the layers used to construct the floor start to separate from one another.

Kits are available to fix floor delamination if need be, so it's not quite the disaster it sounds.

12 Safety equipment

Every caravan or motorhome should be fitted with a fire extinguisher and/or fire blanket for obvious reasons. If you haven't got one, you should purchase one forthwith.

A smoke detector and carbon monoxide alarm are also essential pieces of kit for any leisure vehicle.

Assuming you already have these items the following checks should be carried out:

☑ Check that the fire extinguisher is in good condition, secure, and that the gauge is reading full pressure (in the green area).

☑ Check the extinguisher is suitable for the types of fire that might occur in leisure vehicles – this is usually ABC Dry Powder.

☑ Check the date of the extinguisher. On the model pictured the date is stamped on the case, but on other models

12-1. This extinguisher has full pressure.

it might be on the neck of the extinguisher, or on a printed label.

☑ The service life of an extinguisher is around ten years, after which time it should be replaced.

☑ Check the condition of the fire blanket, that it is still within its case, and the pull chord is visible.

☑ Check that the batteries in the carbon monoxide alarm are still good by depressing the test button: if all is in working order the alarm will sound.

12-2. This extinguisher is dated 2016.

13 The water and sanitary systems

Water and waste tanks

Caravan owners will most likely have portable water and waste tanks, but if you have a motorhome with under-slung water and/or waste tank, check that the tanks are secure, and that any retaining straps or brackets are in good condition.

Many years ago, in one of my first motorhomes the water tank straps decided to give way while I was driving on a dual carriageway and, believe me, it was very frightening and not recommended.

Also, if you haven't done it recently I would recommend treating the fresh water tank with a purifier to make sure the water comes through clean and potable (fit for consumption).

I use 'Puriclean,' which does the job and is relatively inexpensive.

The flushing and purifying of the water tank is not officially part of the habitation check, and if you were having the check done by a professional, this service may be offered, but it will be at extra cost.

For the purposes of the next check I'm going to assume that you've followed my recommendation and added a purifier to the water tank. It would be sensible to clean the tank and water outlets at the same time.

13-1. Puriclean water purifier.

Whether or not you've flushed the tank, check the following with regards to the function of the water system:

☑ Check the water flow is constant and not continually sputtering.
☑ Check the shower head is clean and the spray pattern is good (if fitted).
☑ Check the filters. Water system filters should be changed regularly.
☑ Check the sinks are secure and the shower tray is not damaged or leaking.

☞ If the water flow is sputtering, check the water pipes for kinks or damage to possibly avoid replacing the pump unnecessarily.

Toilets

There are two main types of toilet used in caravans and motorhomes: cassette and portable.

13-2. A cassette toilet with underneath locker access.

Cassette toilets are permanent fixtures inside the vehicle, and have a hatch on the outside of the vehicle so that the waste cassette can be removed and emptied at the disposal point.

Portable toilets do exactly as it says on the tin (as they say), and can be stowed away while travelling, and positioned in a place around the caravan or motorhome at your convenience (sorry for the pun; couldn't resist it!) when on-site.

These units need very little maintenance apart from cleaning and topping up with the correct flush and waste tank liquids.

So, toilet checks only really relate to cassette type toilets

It goes without saying that protective gloves should be worn when cleaning or carrying out maintenance of toilets.

☑ Check the physical condition of the toilet and that it is securely fixed in position.
☑ Check the flush operation.
☑ Check that the waste cassette can be easily removed, and locks back securely into the unit.
☑ Check the cassette level indicator is working properly.
☑ Check the cassette seal is in good condition (not dry and cracked), and lubricate with olive oil if necessary.

13-3. A typical portable toilet.

13-4. Cassette toilet seals can be replaced.

New seals are available for cassette toilets and can be replaced easily and inexpensively. New seals are also available for some portable toilets, depending on the model.

And finally ...
If you're not feeling very pleased with yourself right now then, trust me, you should be – because you're done!

Checking toilets was your last task. So, I can only hope you've enjoyed the book and found it useful, because the last thing I would want is for us to say goodbye on a bum note (sorry!).

Now it's time to grab that beer from the fridge and relax ...

HABITATION AREA SERVICE SHEET

SHEET IS FOR GUIDANCE & DIY USAGE ONLY

PERIODICAL SYSTEMS TESTING BY A QUALIFIED TECHNICIAN IS RECOMMENDED

IF IN DOUBT CONTACT YOUR LOCAL TECHNICIAN OR DEALER

NOTES FOR GUIDANCE

CHECKING FOR DAMP - CHECK AREAS AROUND WINDOWS, ROOFLIGHTS, DOORS & INSIDE LOCKERS/CUPBOARDS

USE THE SEPARATE DAMP REPORT SHEET WHEN RECORDING YOUR RESULTS

GAS LEAK TESTING - NO NAKED LIGHTS/FLAMES! GAS AT BOTTLE MUST BE ON & GAS AT ALL APPLIANCES OFF

CHECK HOSES, PIPES & UNIONS. IF YOU SUSPECT A LEAK TURN OFF GAS & CONTACT A QUALIFIED GAS ENGINEER

FRIDGE - UNIT WILL TAKE A FEW HOURS TO REACH FULL OPERATING TEMPERATURE

ELECTRICAL SYSTEMS - RCD=RESIDUAL CIRCUIT DEVICE & MCB=MINI CIRCUIT BREAKER

IF IN DOUBT CONTACT A QUALIFIED ELECTRICIAN

WATER PUMP & TAPS - REFER TO VEHICLE DATA FOR WINTERISATION PROCEDURE

READ & FOLLOW MANUFACTURERS INSTRUCTIONS & FAMILIARISE YOURSELF WITH EACH TESTER BEFORE USE

USE A PENCIL TO RECORD YOUR RESULTS SO THAT YOU CAN REUSE THIS SHEET EACH YEAR   DATE

DAMP TEST				GAS LEAK TEST	
AREA TESTED	RESULTS			AREA TESTED	RESULTS
	TEST ROOF, WINDOWS, DOORS & INSIDE OF LOCKERS				TEST AT PIPES, HOSES, UNIONS & APPLIANCES

FRIDGE COOLING TEST				12 & 240 VOLT ELECTRICAL SYSTEMS TEST	
START TEMP.	TEMP. AFTER 1 HOUR RUNNING			BATTERY, CHARGER, RCD, MCB's & MAINS SOCKET	
	ALLOW A FEW HOURS FOR FULL OPERATION				TREAT BATTERY TERMINALS WITH BATTERY GREASE

DOORS, WINDOWS, LOCKERS & BLINDS				CHECK OPERATION OF WATER PUMP & TAPS	
CHECK LOCKS, HINGES, STAYS & CATCHES				NEVER RUN PUMP WITHOUT WATER IN THE TANK	
LUBRICATE WITH PENETRATING OIL AS NECESSARY				OPEN SINK TAPS FULLY FIRST TO CLEAR SYSTEM OF AIR	

CHECK TOILET FLUSH & CASSETTE SEAL (IF FITTED)

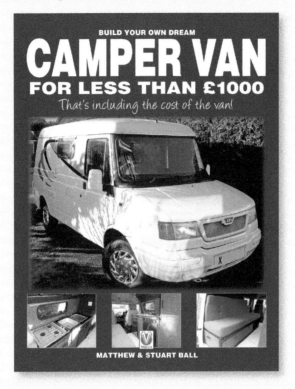

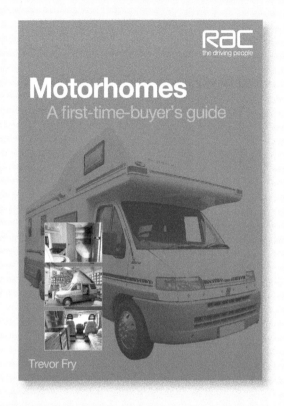

Introducing the wide range of motorhomes and campervans available, this book helps you to make a considered choice that suits both your budget and your needs. Covering new and used markets, written in plain english, and with full colour photographs throughout, this book explains all you need to know for safe, happy motorcaravanning.

ISBN: 978-1-845844-49-3
Paperback • 21x14.8cm • 80 pages • 109 colour and b&w pictures

For more information and price details, visit our website at
www.veloce.co.uk • email: info@veloce.co.uk • Tel: +44(0)1305 260068

Index